Memories in Focus

N.E. Ulster from
old photographs
1860 - 1960

Volume Three

Compiled & Edited
by Tom McDonald
& Robert Anderson

ISBN 0 948154 20 9

Published by Impact Printing, Stone Row, Coleraine
with assistance from the
Arts Council of Northern Ireland

INTRODUCTION

The very idea of "Memories in Focus" running to three volumes would have been dismissed by us as impossible a few years ago. The wealth of old photographs of the area which remained unpublished, however, led us on to Volume Two and now, unbelievably — Volume Three, with sufficient reserves to undertake Volume Four in the future.

With this current volume we have remained within the same geographical boundaries but have included a few photographs as recent as the 1960s. As many sweeping changes have taken place in the past 25 years we feel that the modern generation and those yet to come should have a record of the area as it has appeared in recent decades.

We have also drawn on the large collections of photographs held by the N.E.E.L.B. Library Headquarters in Ballymena and the Irish Room, Coleraine, the Ulster Museum and the Ulster Folk and Transport Museum, Belfast. Having deliberately avoided using these in the first two books we now believe these collections to be less well-known than we first appreciated. Photographs by professionals such as Lawrence, Welch, Hogg and Green are of outstanding quality and interest adding greatly to the private collections also used.

Once again the help given by certain individuals has been immense and totally unselfish. Without help from friends such as those mentioned in the acknowledgements a work of this type would not be practical.

R. A. & T. McD.
1986

DEDICATION

To the photographers and collectors who had the foresight
to record and retain the visual social history of our area.

ACKNOWLEDGEMENTS

Our thanks to the following organisations and individuals without whose help and co-operation on a vast scale our work would not have been possible.

Roy Anderson .... Coleraine
Robert W. Bacon .... Coleraine
Danny Cameron .... Coleraine
Tommy Chestnutt .... Coleraine
Bobbie Clyde .... Coleraine
Cahal Dallat .... Ballycastle
Charlie Hamill .... Coleraine
Hugh Kane .... Portstewart
John Jamieson .... Portstewart
Wm. F. Lake .... Coleraine
James McAfee .... Ballycastle
W. McCaughan .... Ballycastle
J. A. McDonald .... Coleraine
Hugh McGrattan .... Portrush
Dan McLaughlin .... Coleraine
Mrs. F. Pegg .... Portstewart
David Speers .... Bushmills
Malcolm Templeton .... Ballymena
Old Bushmills Distillery (W. McCourt and Claire Balmer)
Ulster Museum (J. N. H. Nesbitt and Staff)
Library H.Q. Ballymena (Lynn McFetridge and Staff)
Irish Room, Coleraine (Lylla Boyd and Marjorie Geary)
Folk and Transport Museum
Coleraine Harbour Commissioners (Will Dalzell)
Royal Portrush Golf Club (Mrs. Stevenson)
Coleraine Chronicle

COLERAINE

TRANSPORT

SURROUNDING AREAS

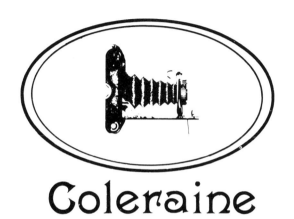

Coleraine

Killowen

Plate 1

The skyline of the west side of the Bann is broken only by St. John's R.C. Church and Hazelbank Farm, while nearer the shoreline is Killowen Primary School (now the Orange Hall) and the Church of Ireland. Before the Reformation the Catholic Church of the Parish of Killowen was situated within the precincts of the present Anglican Church Graveyard and for some years after the present chapel was built in 1834, with the provision of its own burial place, Catholics of the Parish were still buried in the Protestant graveyard. One grave, discovered about 100 years ago, had the body laid in the opposite direction to those surrounding it. It was claimed that this was the resting place of "Friar MacManus", dating from 1798.

Gribbon's Mill

Plate 2

The major source of employment on the west side of the Bann from 1857, when Edward built this weaving factory in Strand Road, were the Gribbon family. Edward's grandfather had been involved in soap making, yarn dealing and the manufacture of both linen and cotton goods on hand-looms since the late 18th century. In 1904 there were 223 looms in operation and four years later an extension was built to house a further 80 machines. Almost 300 people were employed at this time and many families moved to Killowen from rural areas. The closure of the firm in 1925, brought about by spiralling costs, caused considerable hardship among the population of the area, who, for almost three generations, had been fully employed.

Shuttle Hill

Plate 3

A row of modest, single-storey workmen's homes in Shuttle Hill, Killowen. The street derived its name from the weaving industry which was carried on in the area. The houses consisted of a living room and bedroom downstairs with a ladder leading to an attic bedroom. A large range or an open fireplace were used for heating and cooking. In later years Maggie Johnston's shop occupied a central position in this row. The photograph was taken in the 1960s before major development took place and these outdated dwellings made was for modern housing. (see Vol. 2 Plate 26).

Captain Street (Lower)

Two rare photographs from the comprehensive Welch Collection illustrating both sides of Lower Captain Street in the late 1880's. The thatched cottages remained for another 10 or 12 years before making way for Hamilton Terrace and Russell Terrace on the north side and Springmount Terrace and Ashbrook Terrace on the south. Springmount is believed to have derived its name from the well-known constant source of spring water seen in one of the photographs. Most of the whitewashed houses are single-storey with a "loft" bedroom. The householders would draw their water from the spring and sanitation was non-existent. Although outwardly picturesque by today's standards, a report of the 1850s in the local Press strongly condemned the lack of sanitary arrangements in Captain Street, Killowen Street, Dunlop Street, all on the west side of the Bann and in the Clothworker's Estate.

Jackson Hall

Plate 6

A house prominent in Coleraine history is Jackson Hall. The first house to be erected on this site, which was the location of Coleraine Castle in Norman times, was built in 1680. The name Jackson Hall derived from the family who built the house. The Jacksons were the tenants of this section of the Clothworkers' Estate. They were also active in politics over many years. The house was improved in the late 1700's but by the early 1800's had fallen into a state of disrepair. £2000 was spent on renovations by a Mrs. Maxwell, then tenant, in 1824. Later known as the Manor House it was occupied by Blair Stirling, Hugh T. Barrie, M.P. and D. H. Christie. After being sold to the County Council it was used as offices and a clinic until demolished in 1984.

Coleraine Harbour

Plate 7

Taken in early March, 1911, this photograph shows the harbour facilities at the time. The small size of the vessels using the port is apparent from the fact that there are six ships berthed along the quay. In the foreground is the puffer *Saxon*. The name 'puffer' comes from the noise made by the single-cylinder engine. Behind the *Saxon*, on the outside of the row of three ships, are the sister ships *Tosca* and *Shiela* belonging to Mrs. G. A. Smith, of Ayr. *Tosca*, built in 1908, was sunk by the submarine *HMS Sahib* in the Mediterranean in 1943 while under the Italian flag. *Shiela* was wrecked off Land's End in 1921. Other vessels in the photograph are *Loch Doon*, *Brigadier* and *Carlingford Lough*, which were all regular traders to the port.

Customs House

Plate 8

Looking up Bridge Street towards the Diamond in the early 20th century this photograph highlights the buildings on the north side. On the corner of Bridge Street and Circular Road is David Kennedy's drapery shop originally built in 1783 as the Customs House for the port of Coleraine. The building was described in the 1835 Ordnance Survey memoir as being in bad repair held together only by strong bars of iron. The building is today still in existence and occupied by Huey and Henderson. Other premises visible include Henry's Emporium, The Queen's Arms Hotel (See Vol. 2 Plate 2) and the Belfast Bar. The Orr Memorial Fountain at the Diamond had been erected in 1880. The Orr Family ran the Queen's Arms hostelry and posting establishment.

Coleraine Co-Op

Plate 9

The Coleraine Co-Operative Society was started shortly after the first World War by local railwaymen. During its 50 year's existence the Society operated a large grocery shop in Bridge Street, Coleraine, and a fleet of mobile grocery vans and bread vans which were initially horse-drawn until the arrival of motor vehicles. The shop in the photograph was later occupied by the electrical firm Burns and Maguire when the Co-Op moved to larger premises still in Bridge Street. The Society finally closed its doors on 28th November, 1966, and went into voluntary liquidation with sufficient funds to ensure that all debts and share-holders were paid in full. The premises then occupied by the Society were taken over by McConkey and Gould. Those in the photograph which dates from the 1930's are, from left George Parker, Evan Cox and Lewis Thompson.

Bann Rowing Clubhouse

Plate 10

This is a view of a former clubhouse of the Bann Rowing Club. The first boathouse was a wooden structure built in 1864 and it burned down the same year. A brick building was then erected and a storey added in 1881. The existing clubhouse, with a half-timbered upper storey, dates from 1900. A very popular sport in the town, as far back as 1844 the club offered racing boats for sale and in 1905 there was a torchlight procession to celebrate rowing successes, with five bands taking part. The gate lodge entrance to Bannfield House, once the home of Samuel Lawrence, can be seen at the far end of Hanover Place. The chimneys on the skyline are those of Lawrence's Mill, the Bann Steam Saw Mills, (see Vol I. Plate 24) and the gasworks.

Ferryquay Street

Plate 11

Ferryquay Street is undoubtedly one of the oldest streets in the town leading as it did to the ferry quay across the River Bann before the existence of the bridge. Its surroundings at various times in recent history would have included the Monastery, a brewhouse and a malting house. A poor house was situated at the top of the street which had been reconstructed by the Marquis of Waterford in 1830 and was used a few years later as a cholera hospital during a severe epidemic. One of the doctors practising in this period was the famous Dr. Lever. Rothesay House was built on this site and it was later used as rural council offices before being demolished to make way for the present Rothesay Court Complex. The top floor of the wooden warehouse at the bottom right of the street was well known as the YMCA and fun fairs and circuses were occasionally held on the plot of ground alongside.

Gasworks

Plate 12

Despite strenuous opposition from Samuel Lawrence, of Bannfield House, and Dr. Huston, of Rothesay House, the town commissioners erected a gasworks in Hanover Place in 1845 with a mortgage on the town's property. The undertaking served Portstewart and later Portrush as well as the town. It extended south over the years taking in the area known as the Fair Hill. Originally extracting gas from coal imported through the nearby port it was common at this time for coke to be purchased by local householders. The large retort on the left of the photograph was demolished in the 1960's and naphtha, an oil by-product was then used for gas production.

Methodist Church

Plate 13

A panoramic view across the Bann in the late 1880's showing the Methodist Church and Manse in Circular Road and the modest harbour facilities at that time. Methodism is one of the oldest religions established in Coleraine. In 1778 a wing of the old barracks at the Queen's Arms Hotel was converted into a hall. In 1799 a new site was obtained and church and manse built in 1802. This served until the buildings in the photograph were erected in 1854. The architect was Isaac Farrell, of Dublin, who was also responsible for the C.A.I. buildings. Built by Samuel Kirkpatrick, of Coleraine, the original plans are still preserved in the Church. The manse has recently been demolished. The steamer at the quay is the Laird Line's *Fern* which operated a regular service from Coleraine to Glasgow.

Queen Street   Plate 14

A rare view of the junction of Circular Road, Millburn Road and Queen Street, with The Mall on the right, taken in the early 1950's. In 1834 the only road to Portstewart was by way of Brook Street. The hills there made it inconvenient, and at times dangerous in winter. By early 1840's a new road was constructed from The Diamond down Preachinghouse Lane as Queen Street was then known, and by bridging two small streams the new thoroughfare was completed. The railway bridge, which formerly existed to carry traffic from Coleraine Harbour to the main line, can be seen in the background. The three-storey block between The Mall and Circular Road, Castleview Terrace, was demolished shortly after this photograph was taken. A common sight at that time was the small boy coming from the nearby coalyard with a hundredweight bag of coal through the bar of his bicycle.

Corporation Arms Hotel

Plate 15

An architecturally distinguished corner of the Diamond highlighting the Belfast Bank and the Corporation Arms Hotel. The Belfast Bank was built in 1894 of roughly dressed sandstone and is today one of the few Victorian landmarks in the town centre. Prominently displayed on the balcony is the crest of the Coleraine Corporation. Alongside the bank is the once renowned Corporation Arms Hotel. Previously the site of a ladies' school, it was the best known hotel in the town boasting 19 bedrooms, stabling for 16 horses, coach house, car sheds, cowhouse, piggery, field and garden. The other major hotel was the Clothworkers' Arms in Waterside. Both operated carriage services for customers to and from the Railway Station.

Church Street

Plate 16

A striking view of Church Street taken by Robert Welch from the roof of the Town Hall about 1915. Perhaps the most significant feature of the photograph is the absence of traffic of any description on the road near the Town Hall. The road itself appears to be very roughly made up and walkways can be seen across Church Street and at the junction of New Row. The corner blocks are occupied by Anderson's Emporium on the right above which for a time was the town library staffed by Miss Given, sister of town clerk and local historian, Max Given, and by Moorhead's drapery shop on the left with the sunshades extended. Large wooden crates sit outside Moorheads having probably just arrived from the harbour or the railway station.

Bridge Street Looking West   Plate 17

A matching view of the Diamond looking west towards Bridge Street, the Bridge and Waterside. Businesses prominent in the photograph are from left: Hughes Brothers, butchers; Birmingham and Sheffield Warehouse, hardware and fancy goods; Bishops, bootmaker and a public house on either side of Bridge Street. Horse drawn traffic seen in the street includes two jaunting cars in front of the Queen's Arms Hotel. The distant skyline is almost completely agricultural land, housing on the west bank being confined to Captain Street and Killowen. Bishops, established in 1840, continues to carry on business having expanded to occupy almost the whole of the block in the left foreground.

Crawford's Interior

Plate 18

The Crawford family commenced business in The Diamond in the middle of the last century as wholesale ironmongers. The business developed rapidly to include furniture manufacture and upholstery. This pre-1920 interior view of one of their warehouses illustrates the wide range of goods available. Included in the photograph are marble fireplaces, bamboo hall stands, rocking chairs, display cabinets, wardrobes, overmantels, oil lamps, bicycles and cane easy chairs. Many of the items, commonplace when the photograph was taken almost 70 years ago, would command high prices today. An old job docket, in the possession of the Crawford family, shows a mahogany bureau bookcase taking 65 hours to make, 30 to polish and selling for £16 16s 0d.

Flax Market

Plate 19

Cart-loads of flax were a common sight in the Diamond at the regular Saturday market at the turn of the century. This crop was grown extensively by small farmers to supplement their meagre income. When loaded on the cart there followed a slow, arduous journey, often involving many miles, on poor roads. Our photograph shows carts on the north side of the Diamond (or Market Place) behind which groups of farmers and buyers are 'dealing' while two boys, one barefooted, take an avid interest in the photographer. The linen industry, for which flax was grown, was one of the major employers in the North of Ireland. Coleraine had its outlet in Gribbon's Weaving Mill, in Killowen. The flax was also weighed and baled at the Newmarket Street yard for the rail journey to Belfast.

Evening Street Scene

Plate 20

The gas lighting of business premises and street lights at the corner of Bridge Street, Queen Street and The Diamond highlight a wet evening in Coleraine in the early 1900's. On the left MacLaughlin's public house offers a warm and welcoming refuge from the rain. A popular drink then was stout which could be purchased at 2d per pint. Premises next door were occupied by Daniel MacLaughlin, practising as a solicitor in the town since 1872. As a town commissioner he advocated that Coleraine should be made the county town and county buildings provided here. He also wrote a history of the family church, St. John's Killowen. The MacLaughlin family have played a prominent role in the civic life of the town for four generations.

W. J. Baxter's Shopfront

Plate 21

The shopfront of Sir William Baxter's wholesale and retail chemist and grocer, Church Street. A recent delivery is being moved from the kerbside into the shop in the early 1900's. An unusual combination of dispensing chemist and grocer, Baxters also offered photographic equipment and services which included the free use of a darkroom. In a town guide published in 1909 by Wefers, newsagent and bookseller, The Diamond, Baxters advertised 'prescriptions accurately compounded.' The grocery department boasted 'replete with the finest teas, coffees, sugars, table delicacies and provisions for the household.' Sir William's apprentices lived on the premises in the care of a matron and a short religious service was held each morning.

Rosemary Lane Hoarding

Plate 22

An unusual composition by local amateur photographer and businessman, Tom Bellas, taken in 1900, showing the Church Street end of Rosemary Lane, later named Park Street. The power of advertising is apparent here with the gable end of James Nevin's tobacconist shop totally covered in messages from manufacturers of sauce, beer, coffee and 'Force'. Also pasted on the wall are posters detailing emigrant sailings to North America. The front of the shop itself carries a considerable number of signs though most are for the products sold. Mr. Nevin has even gone to the extent of having his name embroidered on a flag. The Coleraine coat of arms has been painted on the wall between the windows on the first floor.

McGilligan's Grocer's Shop

Plate 23

Situated in New Row, close to the junction with Church Street and Rosemary Lane, is McGilligan's grocery shop. Together with Church Street and the Diamond, New Row was also the location for early, small plantation timber frame houses. It has recently been discovered that the building containing McGilligan's grocer's shop was one of these original buildings and roof trusses and other timbers will be featured in a reconstruction at the Ulster Folk Museum. New Row was described by Rev. Sampson in the early 19th century as 'the only place of respectability' off the main thoroughfare. It was also the location of the residence of Sir Tristram Beresford, one of the original agents for the Irish Society. The Beresford name still survives in street names in the town.

New Row

Plate 24

One of the oldest commercial streets in the town, photographed about 1900, appears almost deserted yet housed a wide variety of businesses which attracted many people to New Row. Among these were W. Abraham, agricultural implements; Richard Hunter, auctioneer, whose covered market yard hosted a weekly sale; Craigs, bakers, Stanleigh's, cycle shop, Bates' fruit shop, Central Dining Room and R. W. Jewell, cork cutter. There were no public houses in New Row at a time when they were listed in practically every other street in the town.

Waterlow Market

Plate 25

Waterlow Market stood at the junction of Upper New Row and Dunmore Street. It was erected in 1877 with the intention of providing a suitable alternative site for the various stall holders who crowded the Diamond selling items as varied as fish, old clothes, fruit and hardware. Named after Sir Sydney Waterlow, of the Irish Society, the market was successful for many years before it fell into decline. It had been used as a council storeyard and for a time housed the town fire brigade. The sounding of the fire alarm, which consisted of a siren and whistle located at the gasworks, quite often brought hordes of locals on to the street to follow the appliance even in the early hours of the morning. The whole area has recently been re-developed but a town market is to-day still held on the same site.

Newmarket Street

Plate 26

A cart-lined Newmarket Street photographed about 1910. The street took its name from the new market erected by the Corporation in 1829 and which replaced the old market house in the Diamond. The original name of the street was Boyd Street, called after Dr. John Boyd who owned land in the area. The northern side of the street, opposite the market, was occupied by public houses which provided stabling for horses and rooms where sales and bargains could be completed by those attending the markets. The market itself cost £2783 to erect and the local agricultural show was held here before the advent of the Showgrounds on Ballycastle Road. At the other end of the street Dr. Boyd leased land to John Rennie which was to become the site for the distillery.

Hamill's Coachworks

Plate 27

A relatively modern view of the interior of Hamill's Coachworks, Coleraine, a firm which had been established in Limemarket Street in 1895. The coachworks specialised in the building of gigs, jaunting cars, and other commercial horse-drawn vehicles progressing in time to the construction of caravans, mobile shops and other customised vans and lorries. This photograph was taken in the early 1960s when most of the painting was done by brush for a better finish and when a new Vauxhall Victor cost only £500. Included in the photograph are C. H. Hamill, proprietor, Hugh Daly, Tommy McCloskey, John Kerr, Wilfred Blair, Desmond Campbell, Maeve McGuigan and Robert Hill.

Irish Society Schools

Plate 28

One of the most obvious and lasting influences of the Hon. The Irish Society in Coleraine is their involvement in education. This photograph shows the primary school as rebuilt in 1867/69. The two-storied headmaster's house, which includes a turret, formed part of the original school and was built in 1821 at a time when the site was in use as a bowling green and recreation ground and attracted strong opposition from the local population. The buildings were further extended in 1935 by the well-known local architect Malcolm McQuigg. The Society had originally founded a school for 130 boys and 130 girls in 1705 but this had fallen into disuse in 1739 and was discontinued. This building ceased to be used as a primary school in 1976.

Kennedy's Foundry

Plate 29

The building in the photograph, situated at the corner of Terrace Row and Mountsandel Road, housed a very important and successful business in Victorian times. It was Kennedy's Foundry, which commenced trading here in 1842 casting grate backs, wheels, iron railings, gates and plough mountings. Thirty years later they were employed in the production of barn threshing machines and churning machines, supplying these throughout Counties Londonderry and Donegal. This building was erected in 1876 together with Ardbana House and heralded the manufacture of the world-famous 'Empress' water turbine which was reliably applied to corn threshing, flax spinning, saw milling and bleaching. Other horse traction farm equipment was made at the foundry but the advent of the tractor saw the demise of the firm in the late 1950s.

Smyth's Shop

Plate 30

Frontage of a Coleraine draper's shop in the 1930's, that of Robert Smyth, on the corner of Church Street and New Row. The firm was founded in 1928 when the premises were also the home of the Smyth family. The store extended over the years to take in the upstairs living accommodation, then the adjoining public house and fish shop in Church Street and in later years the former premises of J. J. Maclean in New Row. These particular premises were once the Coachman's Inn, original meeting place of the Route Hunt. A disastrous fire in 1977 meant rebuilding the whole block. The photograph shows Mr. Robert Smyth with his assistants Misses Cowan and Pollock.

Bell House Lane   Plate 31

Formerly named Thompson's Lane, after a well-known Coleraine family, the street later became Bellhouse Lane. The terrace of houses in the photograph were built during the 1870's and were occupied for over 100 years. In the 1840's this small street was one of several in Coleraine having a reputation for disease and insanitary conditions even though it was only a pace away from the town's main thoroughfare. 'Bellhouse' comes from the nearby curfew bell, which was situated on the corner house of that street, formerly the old courthouse of Coleraine. The bell was sounded at 9.00 p.m. and 5.45 a.m. At that time watchmen were employed during these hours 'preventing midnight flittings by debtors and giving warnings about fires.' Total expense for the watchmen in 1861 was £230, the major part of the town's expenses of £377.

Plantation Houses

Plate 32

Dwarfed between larger and more modern premises in this 1930's view are some of the last examples of the 17th century timber framed buildings which, in the Plantation period, formed a continuous terrace on the south side of Church Street. These two shops, 9/10 Church Street, were finally demolished along with adjacent buildings on he left, to make way for new development. Box framed terrace houses, erected between 1610 and 1620 from oak timber forested at the South of County Londonderry, were unique to Coleraine forming as they did the major parts of the principal streets of the town. Recent renovations at a site on the right of this photograph have revealed timber remnants, of buildings entirely erected with mortice and tenon joints on wood cut down in 1585. (See Vol. 1 Plate 18; Vol. 2 Plate 15).

Donkeys in Town

Plate 33

A well-remembered local character, Tim Lamont, affectionately known as 'Limpy' seen here in Church Street, Coleraine, leading two young donkeys. The animals changed hands at times for as little as 10s. each. Behind Tim is a well-known businessman, Danny McGrath, whose family were associated with the butchery business in the town for many years. Across the street, in front of Anderson and Stewart's public house, are parked Morris 8 and Ford Popular cars. Family cars could be purchased then for just over £200 and road tax was a modest £15. Top speeds were advertised at 50 — 55 m.p.h.

Kingsgate Street/Church Street   Plate 34

The point at which Society Street joins Kingsgate Street/Church Street pinpoints the location in the old town ramparts of the 'King's Gate', one of two named gates which provided access through the fortifications. The photograph shows two grocers shops which were to serve the population for many years. Maclean and Wilson & Neill (see Vol. 2 Plate 13) stand alongside a drapers, a restaurant and a public house (see Vol. 1 Plate 16). Beyond Society Street entrance, one of the famous timber framed buildings with its unique piazza, erected in the 17th century by the Irish Society, is occupied by Johnny Blair's greengrocers shop. (see Vol. 2 Plate 15).

Boys' Brigade in Kingsgate Street

Plate 35

The Boys' Brigade proudly march in Kingsgate Street about 1912. Leading is the 1st Company attached to St. Patrick's Parish Church. This particular company has the unique distinction of only having had five captains since its formation in 1893. The organisation was extremely popular with young boys in this period drill nights and parades witnessing the sight of young members dressed in knickerbocker trousers, pill box hats covering short haircuts, shining boots and gaiters and white celluloid collars. Business premises in the background include James Allen, gent's tailor and outfitter; S. J. Moore, chemist; James F. Nevin, tobacconist; Todd's, seed merchant and Haughey's pub across Brook Street, while on the right another tobacconist and confectioner advertises public billiards rooms.

Anderson's Shoe Shop
Plate 36

The once-familiar green tiled shop front of family footwear specialist Robert Anderson in Kingsgate Street. The title 'Moccasin Shoe Store' derived from the fact that Andersons was the only outlet in Coleraine for this brand of shoe. Mr. Anderson previously served in Blair's shoe shop further along Kingsgate Street before establishing this shop in 1933. Other footwear shops at this time included Bishops, Miss Andersons (later to become Nesbitts), Tylers, Hoods and Grahams. Ladies good quality boots retailed at 7s (35p) and country folk visiting the town often walked barefoot to the outskirts before putting on their shoes. This practice, known as 'Buskin' was to save wear and tear and gave the name to Buskin Burn and Buskin Way, west of the River Bann.

Kingsgate Street

Plate 37

The presence of a photographer in 1910 has evoked considerable interest from a group of locals at the junction of Kingsgate Street, Brook Street and Long Commons. The Brook Street corner has changed considerably in the previous decade with the addition of the complete block containing Nevin's tobacconist shop and Todd's china warehouse. On the opposite side of the street are McKay's newsagency and Griffith's Stores. Other businesses carried on in this street included refreshment rooms, butcher, draper, pharmacy, grocer and several confectioners. Dr. Allison practised here also. Compare this view with those on plates 11, 12 and 15 of Volume 1 all of which date from the early 1900's.

The Long Commons   **Plate 38**

This photograph shows the Salvation Army Temple and a number of houses of varying types and appearance in the Long Commons near its junction with Kingsgate Street in the early 1900's. The street's name has its origins in the fact that it formerly led to 'common' grazing land outside the old town defences. It was even then a busy through road. The Salvation Army Temple had been erected in 1892/94 replacing earlier quarters in Brook Street and Society Street (where the Coleraine Unit had been established in 1886). This hall was established in 1938 and finally vacated for new premises in Ballycastle Road in 1982. The founder of the Salvation Army, General William Booth, visited Coleraine in 1906 and was entertained by H. T. Barrie, M.P. at the Manor house.

Todd's Shop

Plate 39

The shopfront of W. F. Todd, at Reid's Terrace, which was at the top of Railway Road, between Lodge Road and Kingsgate Street. It illustrates an unusual combination of business activities within one shop. It was previously an electrical shop occupied by James Dunlop. Other businesses in Reid's Terrace at this period were Miss Burnett's newsagent, Kings, confectionery, Bob Neely, tailor and E. Millen, gent's hairdresser.

Brook Street Schools

Plate 40

This area, at one time known as Hartford's Corner on Horse Road, is now the site of Brook Street Schools and St. Patrick's Church Hall. Opened in 1871, the building was used through the years as Sunday School, meeting place for church organisations, lantern talks, social evenings and pierrot shows. Local Orange Lodges met in the hall until 1910. The premises were among the first in the area to be marked out for badminton. There was always a billiards room and during the war radar classes were held in the building. At the time of the photograph the caretakers were James and Sarah Cameron. They held this position for over 30 years. The new church hall was built on the site of the small houses in 1964.

Circular Road

Plate 41

This photograph, though fairly modern, is a classic example of what changes can take place to a neighbourhood in what seems almost overnight, when terraces of homes with their own close-knit community, are demolished and replaced by modern houses. This part of the street running from Railway Road to Brook Street, would have housed successive generations of the same families and built up a similar community spirit as that which prevailed in Brook Street, George's Place and Park Street. Before the development of Railway Road, Circular Road was the main route to and from Bushmills and Ballycastle.

Westbrook Hotel   Plate 42

Period dress features prominently among the ladies posed in front of the Westbrook Temperance Hotel in Railway Road around 1910. Temperance was a serious issue in the late 1800's leading to the establishment of cafes, hotels and organisations strictly adhering to abstinence. The Westbrook Hotel is known to have been in existence prior to 1884 at a period when local Presbyterian Church members are recorded as requesting the provision of unfermented wine at communion. Business at the Westbrook would have been enhanced by the hotel's close proximity to the towns railway station.

Royal Visit

Plate 43

The platform at Coleraine railway station provides the setting for a guard of honour of local Boys' Brigade Companies for the Duke and Duchess of York (later King George VI and Queen Elizabeth) during a brief halt on their journey between Londonderry and Belfast on 24th July, 1924. Escorting the Duke is Tommy Glenn of the 1st Company who served as captain from 1904 —1948.

Another important visitor to the local BB fraternity was Sir William Smith, founder of the movement, who inspected Coleraine Companies at the Tip Head football pitch in Brook Street. At this time activities in the companies included rifle drill with dummy weapons of Boer War pattern.

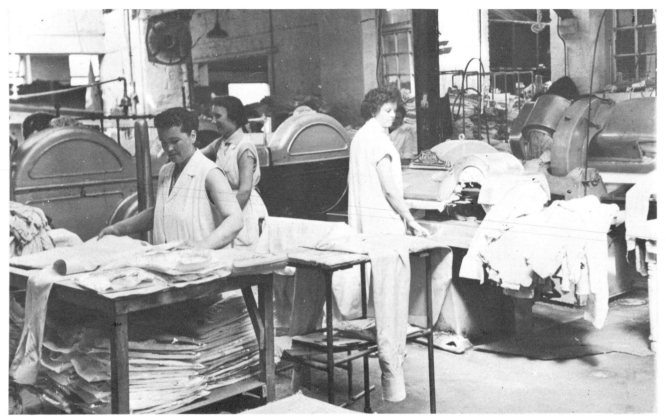

Portrush and Coleraine Laundry

Plate 44

An interior scene of the Portrush and Coleraine Laundry in the late 1950's. The laundry was situated on the corner of Railway Place and Railway Road, the site presently being used as a car park. At this time it handled up to 90,000 items of soiled linen per week this figure increasing substantially during the summer months when hotels and guest houses in the surrounding holiday resorts were extremely busy. Eleven tons of solid fuel were used per week to provide hot water and steam for pressing. Eight familiar blue and white vans served areas as far away as Strabane and Portadown. Some older employees recollected that in 1918 they were often required to work from 7.00 a.m. — 10.00 p.m. for 2½d (1p) per hour.

Westbrook Terrace   **Plate 45**

The summer fashion in 1912 is evident in this group, mainly of ladies, taking part in a 'Catch My Pal' parade. Full skirts and high necks topped off with ornate, wide brimmed hats are popular despite the obvious good weather. The overhead gantry, part of the railway signalling apparatus can be seen in the background. Also prominent in the background is a square chimney in R. & J. Young's timber yard, where steam power would have been required to operate the machinery.

Prefabs

Plate 46

Emergency prefabricated housing erected after the Second World War in Windsor Avenue by Coleraine Borough Council to provide much-needed accommodation for an ever-increasing population. Similar schemes were adopted in James Street, Lambeth Way and Drumadragh. Originally intended as a temporary solution some still remain. In 1963, fifteen years after they were assembled, the local authority considered spending £500 per unit, estimated to increase their lifespan by a further 30 years. This would have led to an increase in rent to 15s (75p) per week. In the event the houses in the town were dismantled and some replaced by more permanent buildings.

Portstewart

Promenade

Plate 47

An extremely early view of the promenade in Portstewart taken around 1870 before any major harbour facilities had been constructed. The double-ended fishing boats seen in the photograph were simply hauled up on the shore to an area cleared of loose stones and boulders. Most of the large houses on the promenade were built between 1833 and 1835. The house on the corner is the site of the present Carrig-na-Cule Hotel. One of the major landowners in the area, Henry O'Hara, built the large house known as the Castle in 1834 at the opposite end of the town. Both local landowners encouraged building in the resort in an effort to establish Portstewart as a 'watering place' for town and city folk.

Harbour Scene   **Plate 48**

This view of the harbour and promenade dates just over a decade into the 20th century when a large number of Portstewart families still depended on the sea for their livelihood. There are at least twelve large fishing boats and numerous smaller craft to be seen. The slipway and inner dock were added to the existing harbour facilities in 1910. A few years earlier an application had been made by the Montagu Arms Hotel to obtain a licence to serve alcohol between the hours of 4 and 5 a.m. 'for the benefit of the fishermen.' The request was refused but indicated that a possible demand existed although incomes from fishing were meagre and seasonal. Local grocery merchants, particularly Mr. S. R. Henry of the Carrig-na-Cule, were expected to extend credit outside the fishing season. (See Vol. 1 Plates 48, 49 and 50 and Vol. 2 Plates 45 and 50).

Harbour Dry

Plate 49

Extensions and renovations to the harbour prior to the first World War provide this unique spectacle of a dry harbour. When this photograph is compared with the previous one (and those in Volume 1) the extent of the reconstruction is evident. The area of the inner dock has been practically doubled with the removal of the slipway and quay. Mr. John Cromie, the landowner and occupant of the Cromore Estate, provided the finance for the establishment of the first harbour. As an improving landlord he also built and leased the first hotel, provided good housing and even a bathing establishment and saw the transition of Portstewart from fishing village to seaside resort. Yet he made the controversial decision not to allow the railway access to the town in the belief that its coming would alter the 'select' character of the resort.

Slipway

Plate 50

Always the focal point of the promenade, the harbour has played an important role in the establishment of the town. This early view of the harbour was taken about 1905 before any of the major work undertaken to add the inner dock had commenced. The photograph illustrates the slipway and handwinch used to hoist the boats from the water. The larger boats are at moorings in the dock while yet more are laid up in front of the houses in Harbour place. Harbour facilities at Portstewart were popular with the owners of smaller boats because, unlike Portrush there were no harbour dues as the local landlord had provided the facilities himself.

York Hotel

Plate 51

The demolition of the York Hotel on the Portmore Road, in 1985, saw the end of an era and the removal of a famous landmark. Built in 1903 on a splendid site overlooking the sea and the local golf course, its clientele down the years included many famous figures. It was richly furnished and decorated with antiques and had a beautiful staircase leading to the upper floors. An entrance porch was added later. Visitors in the early years of the century often remained for the season and partook of sea bathing, golf and trips around the coast. Having often arrived by steam train and tram, guests were attended by many servants including bell boy, chambermaid, valet etc. The hotel was originally owned by Mr. Sheridan whose family also had close links with the Causeway Hotels.

Portstewart House

Plate 52

This large town house, standing towards the northern end of the Promenade, was erected by John Cromie as a residence in 1827. The Cromie family, landlords of the Cromore estate, had let Cromore House at this time and presumably lived in Portstewart House. He returned to Cromore in 1834 after making improvements to the house. He died there in 1874 and the estate descended, through the marriage of his daughter, to Lord Robert Montagu. It is ironic that the properties of the two opposing landlords of Portstewart O'Hara and Cromie eventually passed to the Montagus. Portstewart House is today the location of a fashion shop, a bank and a newsagents.

Frizzell's Shop
Plate 53

McGowan's bakers, Seaward House and Frizzell's grocery shop form the background for this 1907 snapshot. The grocer's shop is located on the site of the present McIntyres, newsagency and fancy goods store and displays posters advertising custards, jellies and Eiffel Tower Lemonade at 4d for two gallons. Also hanging outside the shop is a stalk of bananas, which would have been an unusual delicacy at that time. The waggonette awaits golfers and other passengers for its regular journey out to the new Strand Head golf course. Seaward House boarding establishment, run by Mrs. William Frizzell, would have catered for an influx of Scottish holidaymakers during the high season and local middle class clientele in June and September.

Tram Depot

Plate 54

The handsome mock-Elizabethan tram depot situated beside the Montagu Arms Hotel on the Promenade. This replaced a rather mean structure which formerly occupied this site until 1899 when the new depot was constructed in a similar style to Portrush Railway Station. Adjacent is the boot and shoe shop of I. Wilson and Son. Tickets to Cromore Station were sold on the cars by the conductor who passed from car to car while the tram was in motion — a dangerous practice. In 1911, the approximate date of this photograph, the fares were 2d (1p) single and 3d (1½p) return, third class — first class having been abolished. The 1½ mile journey took 15 minutes. (See Vol. 1 Plates 53 and 54).

Crescent
Plate 55

Many changes have taken place at the Crescent since this photograph was taken by R. J. Welch in the late 1920's. Occupying the site of the present town hall, on the left of the picture, are a single-storey cottage and a small two-storey house. The cottage was probably originally thatched and, like the row known as Bone Row underneath the Castle, among the first buildings erected in the town. The large houses were built mostly by Coleraine businessmen during the 1830's. Still to be developed into the paddling and boating ponds of today the area to the right looks very bare. Charabancs await passengers at the corner and the tramlines turning into the depot building are clearly visible. (See Vol. 1 Plates 55 and 76).

Agherton Church

Plate 56

The clarity of this 1890 view of Agherton Parish Church at the Diamond is remarkable. The church was erected on this site in 1839 and a chancel added in 1879. The tower allowed a space for the eventual fitting of the town's timepiece. The origin of the word 'Agherton' can be traced back to the Norman period. John Cromie, one of the local landlords, build a few fishermen's cottages in the 19th century and from this humble beginning the town developed. He also gave encouragement and finance to support the Parish Church and its then 14 societies. Among changes in the surroundings of the church has been the removal of the small stone-walled cottages on the right. (see Vol. 1 Plate 68).

Golf Clubhouse   **Plate 57**

Ten years after its introduction to the Portstewart Road 9-hole course in 1895, the game of golf received a boost with the decision of the local club to develop a new course at Strand Head. The links were laid out at a cost of just over £1,300 but a new clubhouse was not erected until 1928. Our photograph shows the forerunner of this facility. Golfers in these early years used gutta-percha balls and clubs with names such as "baffy, cleek, jigger and lofter'. Today, these terms would not be recognised.

Burnside Cottages

Plate 58

Our early 1950's view of Burnside village showing the terrace of single storey houses which fronted onto what today is known as Strand Road. These small houses were at one time or another occupied by members of the Hemphill, Hayes and Campbell families all long-established in Burnside. The terrace was demolished in the early 1960's at the start of major development which has gone on since. The fields in front of and behind the houses in this photo have all recently seen extensive building work. (See Vol. 1 Plate 74).

Portrush

Metropole Hotel

Plate 59

The Hotel Metropole, at the corner of Salisbury Terrace and Portstewart Road, built before the First World War, was a popular venue for visitors despite its location outside the town. The resort had grown from a few stone-built cabins, tenanted by fishermen and pilots in 1800, to a respectable Victorian watering place after the arrival of the railway in the 1850's and the establishing of regular steamship services the mainland. The popularity of Portrush harbour as a departure point, a holiday resort and with the establishment of golf courses all encouraged the development of hotels in the town. The Metropole has latterly served as Ulster Savings Branch offices from the beginning of World War Two until the late 1960s and is now an old people's home.

Golf Competition

Plate 60

Open Championship competitions for both male and female golf enthusiasts were a regular feature of the Royal Portrush Golf Club. This photograph shows one such competition on the original course at the turn of the century. The railway played a significant part in the development of the golf club which by the 1930's had moved to the present courses. In 1936 a Golfers' Express operated from Belfast allowing 1st class travel including lunch, use of course and clubhouse with return fare plus dinner on the same day all for 13s 6d. This part of the former course, known locally as the triangle, was played on until 1948. The background shows Coleraine Road, Metropole Hotel and Salisbury Terrace.

Golf Terrace

Plate 61

Directly opposite the first railway station to be developed in the town is Golf Terrace, a row of grandiose three-storied town houses built in the 1880's and 1890s. The golf course at this time was adjacent to this terrace. Their size and convenience to the railway later encouraged many to be developed as guest houses. The R.U.C. station was also located in this row before moving to the present site.

Site of Railway Station

Plate 62

By 1891 the existing railway station, which was situated opposite Golf Terrace was totally inadequate for the heavy summer traffic. A completely new station was opened in the Spring of 1893 and was described as one of the most handsome railway buildings in Ireland. Dating about 1880 our photograph shows the area on which the new station was to be developed. In 1883 Giant's Causeway Tramway commenced operations from this area also. The Town Hall dates from 1872. A branch line to the harbour can be seen in the middle of the photograph. This was opened in June 1866 and no steam engines were permitted to be used on this line until an Act of Parliament rescinded this decision bringing to an end the spectacle of horse-drawn railway wagons.

Station Cafe

Plate 63

In 1893 a red brick and half-timbered Stockbrokers' Tudor-style railway station was opened in Portrush. One wing of the new building housed the cafe and restaurant. This interior view dating from c1905 illustrates the elegance of the era. Patrons were treated to silver service, linen table cloths and napkins, a highly-polished bar, and practical bentwood chairs. The dining-room seated up to 300 and was 90 feet long x 30 feet wide. It was occasionally used as a concert hall. Underneath was considerable storage space and cellars in which liquid refreshments for the Railway Hotel and dining cars was located. Outside was a balcony overlooking the skating rink and gardens with spectacular views of the West Bay and Atlantic Ocean. The entire station complex was built at a cost exceeding £10,000 and the cafe was finally demolished in 1970.

Azalea in Harbour

Plate 64

This busy scene of Portrush Harbour in 1905 is dominated by the Laird Liner steamer *Azalea* about to depart on her regular run to Ardrossan. Built in 1878, for the Dublin to Glasgow run, the ship was later moved to the daylight service from Portrush to Scotland and was a forerunner of the famous *Hazel*. During her career with the Laird Line the '*Azalea*' was involved in two incidents in the Foyle, once when she just managed to avoid a sailing ship which was out of control and again when she collided with a rival firm's ship in the river. The resulting bump, which occasioned only very slight damage, caused dozens of gentlemen thrown out of their bunks by the impact, to appear on deck dressed in their nightshirts. No mention was made of the female passengers' reaction.

Portrush Yacht

Plate 65

The '*La Fone*', a magnificent 43 ton racing yacht owned by Mr. Moore Brown of Portstewart, is the subject of this 1910 photograph taken in Portrush Harbour. He was the tenant of Portstewart Castle at that time and was a well known figure in the yacht racing world. The '*La Fone*' was built in Portrush in 1901 by James Kelly, a local boatbuilder of some repute. Among those on the deck of '*La Fone*' are Billy Carter, caretaker of Portrush Town Hall after retiring from the Royal Navy and Coastguard services and Bob and Willie Gregg of Portrush, who were also boatbuilders. *La Fone*' sank in the North Sea in 1934.

Hurricane Debbie

Plate 66

Portrush Harbour at the height of a 113 miles an hour gale known as 'Hurricane Debbie' on Saturday, 16 September, 1961. The boats in the photograph include Doherty's *Girl Doreen* , Stewart's *Scott* , McMullan's *Cutty Sark* and *Family Friend* . Although under severe strain all the moorings held. The background has undergone consider-able change. Gone are the old railway bridge, Watt's store and much of the terrace on the right. The railway bridge has been replaced, Portrush Yacht Club now occupy Watt's site and Waterworld has been built alongside the Harbour Bar.

Mark Street

Plate 67

Mark Street is named after Lord Mark Kerr, a member of the Antrim family, who were landowners in the Portrush area. The street then consisted of large private houses dating from the late 19th century and were occupied mainly by prominent business and professional people. At the southern end of the street behind the photographer stood the Presbyterian schoolhouse dating from 1860 and now the Simpson Hall. On the seaward side is a steep cliff created by the removal of stone for the harbour.

Portrush Hotel

Plate 68

Replacing a row of thatched cottages the Portrush Hotel was the resort's first purpose-built hotel. Erected in the mid 1800's after the arrival of the railway and the development of Portrush as a watering place it served a middle-class clientele and was somewhat overshadowed by the neighbouring Antrim Arms Hotel which was later to become the Northern Counties. Sam Fawcett developed the business of tour operations from Fawcetts Royal Hotel at a time when it boasted the first electric lift in the area and a sea view from every window.

Northern Counties Dining Room

Plate 69

A share of the lease of the Antrim Arms Hotel was purchased in 1883 by the Northern Counties Hotel Company Limited. The hotel was primarily intended for high-class tourists proceeding to the Causeway. It boasted French cuisine and, as can be seen from the photograph, luxurious surroundings. In 1914 the French waiters and German band at the hotel packed their bags and departed hurling insults at each other. The dining area was enlarged and improved with a cocktail lounge added in 1935/36. The room had an ornate frieze around the ceiling and arches, lace curtained windows, wood-panelled walls and gas lighting. Tables were elaborately laid with linen and silver, cut glass decanters and aspidistra plants complementing leather-upholstered seats and richly carpeted floor.

Princess Street

Plate 70

A rarely photographed area of the resort is Princess Street which joined Lansdowne with Ramore Street. Built in the late nineteenth century by a local man the street was originally named 'Esdale' Terrace after him. It was also earlier known as North Street. The ground to the west was then known as the meadow. This became the popular Recreation Grounds in 1923.

Main Street

Plate 71

Elegant Edwardian ladies and their charges stroll past the imposing Belfast Bank building (left) built in 1897 on the site of a boys' school which was attached to the Holy Trinity Parish Church, the railing of which are clearly visible. The Church, dating from 1842, had these railings removed as part of the war effort almost a century later. On the extreme right is Campbell and Chalmers grocery shop. Many of the buildings in the centre of the photograph were destroyed in the 1976 firebomb attack on the resort.

Main Street Looking North

Plate 72

A scene of activity and general interest of one of the busiest sections of the main thoroughfare of the town. Among the businesses identified on the right are The Orchard Cafe and Public Billiard Room, P. Fusco, the Picture House, Black's Popular Cafe, Lee, photographer, City Hotel, C. McConaghie. The cinema was the first in the resort and survived until the late 1950s. On the left is G. McCann, chemist, Portrush House, Irish Embroidery Depot, Hughes Bros., drapers, in the building which was later to be used by the Northern Bank and Bamford's tearooms. The cart making its way slowly down the street contains wicker baskets and boxes probably of fish.

Original Methodist Church   Plate 73

A very rare view of the original Methodist Schoolhouse and Church which dates from 1832. The Clarke Memorial Church was used on weekdays as a school and on the Sabbath for worship. It was used also by other denominations as a place of worship and the famous Presbyterian minister Rev. Jonathan Simpson was ordained here on Christmas Day, 1842. The church was replaced by the present building in 1887. The chimes of a bell cast in 1603 still ring out as a recording. This bell had been presented to the British Ambassador by the Czar of Russia and eventually made its way to Portrush via Dr. Clarke. The bell is presently preserved inside the church.

Arcadia

Plate 74

Always a focal point of entertainment in Portrush is the Arcadia whose steady development can be traced in postcard scenes down the years. The first substantial building was provided by R. A. Chalmers, a prominent local businessman and council chairman. The balcony above the cafe and fancy goods shop was used for open air dancing. At the side of the shops stand two early forms of amusement — a weighing machine and metal embossing printer. The buildings to the left contain the salmon fishery which has operated since the 1600s. Anchored in the Skerry Roads is a R. N. Destroyer.

Tram at Causeway Street

Plate 75

The tram makes its way down the steep incline of Causeway Street on its way towards the depot, Bushmills and the Giant's Causeway at the turn of the century. A steam engine is being used as at the time a dispute with the local Urban Council about electrification forced the Tramway Company to continue using steam locomotives as far as the tramway depot. Portrush Gaswork beside this depot provided street lighting and domestic supplies within the town although electricity is beginning to make an impact. The couple having a stroll are typical Edwardian holidaymakers.

Kiln-an-Oge Hotel Fire

Plate 76

On the afternoon of 29 May, 1935, the Limekiln at the White Rocks, Portrush — described as one of the finest houses of its type in the district — was completely destroyed by fire. Despite the best attentions of both the Portrush and Coleraine Fire Brigades, who were hampered by lack of water, the building blazed for three hours. Only a few items of furniture were saved. The fire started in the kitchen and a nurse, who was ill in bed, had to be rescued by ladder. It was not a good year for Portrush and its ten volunteer fire-fighters. Only four months later two dwelling houses and a cafe in Main Street were destroyed by an overnight fire. The site of the Limekiln is today occupied by the Kiln-an-Oge Hotel.

Transport

North-West 200 Millburn Hairpin

Plate 77

The 350cc race of the 1947 'North-West 200' and Ken Bills leads Albert Mole and Malcolm Templeton round the famous Millburn Hairpin at Coleraine. Malcolm Templeton went on to win the race at an average speed of 68.03 miles per hour. Normally run in May the 'North West 200' has been the major sporting event in the area since 1929. The course, bikes and speeds have changed dramatically since this photograph. Many other famous names from the annals of motor-cycling history have taken part in what has become the fastest road race in the British Isles. These include George Brockerton, Malcolm McQuigg, Artie Bell, Geoff Duke, Tom Herron and Joey Dunlop.

McGildowney's Pier

Plate 78

An interesting view of McGildowney's pier at Ballycastle, which was erected by Hugh McGildowney of Clare Park in 1891. At the end of the pier the *Glentow* is being loaded by steam crane. This little steamer carried local limestone to Glasgow and returned with coal, pier ponies being used to draw the loads to and from the vessel. The *Glentow* was sunk off Fairhead in 1915. The *Hazel* mentioned in the Portrush section of this series of books, called at Ballycastle Bay as did some of the emigrant ships bound for America. (See Vol. 2 Plate 88).

Bushmills Distillery Lorries

Plate 79

Two lorries from Old Bushmills Distillery Company Ltd await loading by steam crane at Portrush Harbour in 1933. The ship from which the coal is being discharged is *S. S. Rathmore* which belonged to local coal importers J. R. Watt, Ltd. The world-famous Bushmills Distillery was first granted a licence to distil in 1608 and more recently had close connections with Coleraine and Killowen Distilleries. Its product today reaches more than 100 countries through the world and even 200 years ago was being exported to North America and the West Indies.

Henry's Charabancs

Plate 80

The 1920's saw rail travel come under increasing competition from motor transport. One of the earliest forms of alternative travelling was the Thorneycroft charabanc which could carry up to 30 passengers. Although it was noted in later years that many of these vehicles were often unroadworthy, the cheap fares and door-to-door service were attractive benefits. Portstewart to Coleraine was offered the services of three buses operated by P. Doherty while S. R. Henry, who owned the Carrig-na-Cule Hotel, specialised in coastal tours. This view shows two of Henry's charabancs at Henry's Corner, Portstewart, with the tram tracks on the right. S. R. Henry was eventually to become the last manager and also the receiver of The Portstewart Tramway Co. in 1897 when it was purchased by B. and N. C. Railway Co. for £2,100.

Last Train

Plate 81

Coleraine photographer, John Leonard, was present to capture on film the last train to cross the old swing bridge at Coleraine. Built in 1860 to link the two lines terminating in the town, the bridge also had to allow access by ships to the port further upstream. This photograph was taken on 23rd March, 1924, and shows a train approaching Coleraine from Londonderry. Two days previously the first train had used the new £100,000 bridge. This was ten times pre-war estimate. The old bridge was replaced by a new structure just a few hundred yards downstream and was dismantled that year. (See also Vol. 2 Plates 24 and 94).

Ballycastle Narrow Gauge

Plate 82

A steam engine and carriages stand at Ballycastle Railway station before setting off on the 16-mile journey to Ballymoney. The railway ran on 'narrow' (3 ft) gauge instead of the more common 5ft 3 ins. It was opened in 1880 and ran through Capecastle, Armoy, Stranocum and Dervock to Ballymoney main line station. Big days on the little system would have been the 1st July and 1st August, when a large influx of select visitors from Belfast arrived on holiday, and also the late August Lammas Fair. The line closed in 1924 as unprofitable but soon reopened as part of the L.M.S. system. It finally closed on Sunday, 2 July, 1950. Those in the photograph are H. Conway (in carriage) John Bailey, station master (on rails); Jack McDuff and Bob Kilpatrick (in cab) and Pat Duffin.

Aerial Ropeway

Plate 83

During the reconstruction work on the moles at the Barmouth in the 1930's an aerial ropeway or 'Blondin' was erected in order to transport stones and other materials from the Portstewart side of the river to the Castlerock side. The photograph shows the ropeway in operation as a load of stone arrives from the quarry at Carnanee aboard the narrow gauge train in the background. High enough to permit the passage of ships to and from Coleraine the Blondin was occasionally used to transport men across the river. This must have been a nerve-wracking experience indeed as the operators would often make the car bounce as a joke when half-way across the Barmouth.

Vegetable Cart   Plate 84

Mr. Jim Bradley, who operated a horse-drawn fruit and vegetable run round the Coleraine district for many years in the 1940's. The photograph was taken on Strand Road, Coleraine, with the former Clothworker's Hotel in the background then occupied by motor engineers. Douglas.

Town deliveries by horse and cart of coal, milk, bread and vegetables were commonplace until the mid 1950's. Gas street lamp and 'Halt at major road ahead' sign can be seen on the left while an Austin 7 car sits parked beside the Strand Road park.

Steam Steam Steam

Plate 85

This rare photograph of the jetty at Carnanee Quarry, on the River Bann, was taken by Mr. A. F. Chapman, who was Resident Engineer on the Barmouth Improvement Scheme. The date is September, 1929, and the event was the arrival, at the still incomplete jetty, of the narrow gauge steam engines which were to haul the stone-laden wagons from the quarry to the Barmouth. The first of two engines is being lifted from the deck of a small Kelly steamer by the large mobile steam crane which worked on the scheme at both the quarry and at the Barmouth. The improvement scheme at the river entrance lasted from 1929 — 1943.

Carriages at Station

Plate 86

Jaunting car, open carriage and landau in front of Coleraine railway station around 1910. Prospective rail travellers are alighting from a carriage belonging to the Clothworker's Hotel in Waterside. It was common practice for hotels to run such a service for guests in those days. The landau may be arriving from the other major hotel in the town, the Corporation Arms, or from some of the larger estates in the area. The railway station had been opened in 1855 but was almost completely re-built in 1882 by which time the station had links with many parts of the country. Horse-drawn carriages then acted in the role of feeder services to the railway when once they had been the only means of travelling from town to town.

Coal Boat at Portstewart

Plate 87

The harbour at Portstewart must have seemed very small indeed to the crew of the puffer *Sergeant* berthed here about 1912. *Sergeant* is off loading coal and the large bucket used in the operation can be seen near her mast. It is probable that the coal was for Cromore House and arrived from Ayr, in Scotland. The *Sergeant* was built in 1903 for Coasting Steamships, of Glasgow, and was 67 feet long and 18 feet beam. The 95 ton steamer was one of very few commercial vessels to enter Portstewart Harbour. (See Vol. 1 Plates 48 — 51 and Vol. 2 Plate 44).

Coleraine '100' Road Race

Plate 88

A series of motorcycle road races known as the 'Coleraine 100', were held over a circuit taking in Macosquin — Keady — Ringsend in the years 1925/26/27. Our photograph shows a competitor about to set off from the official starting line on the 100 mile race. He is S. Wallace, riding a 2½ h.p. Rex Acme motorcycle and dressed in an early form of racing leathers, crash helmet and goggles. Among the large crowd of spectators is a young Danny Cameron, Coleraine, even then interested in all things mechanical and later to be well-known in many other sporting circles.

Steamers and Sailing Ships

Plate 89

A crowd has gathered on the North Pier at Portrush Harbour to watch the departure of the Laird Lines *Olive* to Ardrossan amidst a cloud of smoke and steam. *Olive* was capable of carrying almost 1000 steerage class and 100 saloon class passengers. Remaining in the harbour are a barquentine off loading timber near the entrance and a two-masted topsail schooner near the old railway bridge. Men can be seen carrying cargo aboard the schooner and all around is evidence of a busy port in the form of railway wagons, piles of timber and coal and many horses and carts. In the middle of the harbour are a large sailing yacht and fishing smacks at moorings.

Doctor's Trap

Plate 90

Dr. Chas. Forsythe, M.D. and his driver Tommy Newton, photographed with their pony and trap outside the Medical Hall in Church Street, Coleraine, in the first decade of the 20th century. Transport was essential since a Coleraine doctor would have covered areas of Dunboe, Macosquin, Aghadowey, Ballyrashane and Agherton treating common maladies such as dyspepsia, influenza, measles and occasionally cholera. For their services doctors charged 5d per visit over four miles distance. Their salary from the practice averaged £50 per year. Next door to the Medical Hall, oddly enough, is situated Long's funeral parlour.

The End of the Line

Plate 91

The Giant's Causeway tram awaits passengers at the Causeway terminus before setting off on the 10 mile journey to Portrush via Bushmills. Three different types of carriage are in operation on this train, the motorised open car at the front with central trolley-pole standard, an early first class saloon and bringing up the rear the third class wagon No. 6 with its storm canvas neatly furled. On the left, illegible in the brilliant evening sunshine is the White House hoarding and in the haze beyond the Bush Bay are the hills of Gortnee where the train faced a long slow haul out of Bushmills before topping the hill at Boneyclassagh and on to the scenery of Dunluce and the Whiterocks.

Harbour Wagons

Plate 92

A crowded scene at Coleraine Harbour as wagon drivers, helpers and dockers pose for a photograph taken in 1951. The photograph shows horse-drawn wagons loaded with bags of potatoes for export from the port. Also evident is the harbour railway which was still very important then and various lorries and cars on the quay. Robert Hunter's coal yard can be seen in the background along with that of Hamiltons and further down the quay the old railway weighbridge is in operation. Potatoes formed a very important part of the trade figures for Coleraine Harbour at this time as both eating and seed varieties were being exported to the mainland.

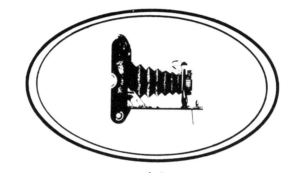

Surrounding Areas

Garvagh Railway Station

Plate 93

A crowded scene at Garvagh Railway Station on the now defunct Derry Central line which operated between Coleraine and Magherafelt during the years 1880 until the 1950's. Such numbers of passengers would only have been evident when special excursion trains were operated to events such as fireworks displays at Portrush. The station, being situated away from the town centre, had two jaunting cars to facilitate customers — one operated by the Imperial Hotel and the other by Hugh Wade. Two long carts delivered goods from the trains and a cattle dock was located nearby. Oil lamps were used as signals and platform staff were required to replenish the oil and trim the wicks.

Castlerock

Plate 94

A view of Castlerock village looking east towards the Bann mouth and Portstewart. The development of Castlerock owes much to the Coleraine to Londonderry railway. Much of the land in the area was given free by local landlord Sir Hervey Bruce who was to become a director of the Belfast and Northern Counties railway company and who stipulated that every train must stop at Castlerock. In May, 1860, the issue of free 'villa tickets' saw an increase in building of large houses in the resort. In order to qualify for villa tickets, which allowed free first-class travel for a period of 10 years, plans for houses which would have a valuation of over £25 had to be submitted to the railway's engineers before building commenced. This scheme lasted for over 60 years.

Castlerock Golf Club

Plate 95

The motor cars in this photograph of Castlerock Golf Club help to date it around 1955. The Edwardian wooden clubhouse, whose design owes much to the architecture of railway stations of the period has been totally renovated in recent years only the clock being incorporated in the new building. Castlerock Golf Club was founded in 1901 under the Presidency of local landlord Sir Hervey Bruce and first club captain Stuart C. Ross J.P. The club was affiliated to the Golfing Union of Ireland in 1903. While the main building has changed dramatically the other smaller structure, which was used as the professional's shop, has been totally removed.

Bushmills Market Square

Plate 96

The market yard and stores in Bushmills were built in 1828 and in 1874 the clock-tower, which dominates this view of Market Square (or the Diamond as it is also known), was added. The market was held each Tuesday, with a grain sale on Fridays during the harvest season. The archway on the left disappeared in 1910 when the building on the near corner was enlarged and became the Working Men's club and Reading Rooms. When the town was provided with mains water the iron railings were removed and a pump installed in the alcove at the base of the tower. A watering trough for horses was provided and on market days both it and the Dining Rooms on the far corner of the market provided refreshment for man and beast.

Ketch at Runkerry

Plate 97

The remarkable sight of a ketch, apparently aground on the beach below Runkerry House, leads to wide speculation about the reason. Littered along the foreshore is round timber which could have been the vessel's cargo. The position of the ship and the exposed nature of the bay points to a stranding rather than a deliberate beaching. Black Rock in the left background was the location of two recorded shipwrecks — the *Petrel* in 1882 and the schooner *Emerald* in 1879.

Causeway Hotel

Plate 98

Built in 1836 the Causeway Hotel has dominated the approaches to the Giants Causeway for one hundred and fifty years. The coming of the tramway in 1897 and the fact that the chief engineer was also an Hotel director provided the Causeway Hotel not only with electric light but also exclusive rights to the conveyance of passengers from the terminus, side-cars from the Royal Hotel being forced to wait on the roadway outside the tramway yard. The decorative pagoda tea-rooms were open late into the summer evenings providing much needed refreshment for those who had sampled the wonders of the coastline.

The Diamond, Ballycastle

Plate 99

Two modes of transport are featured in this view of the Diamond, Ballycastle taken in 1904. A horse and cart stand at the O'Connor Memorial — the animal making full use of the drinking trough provided. The Model T Ford — registration number OI2955, has as a backcloth the long-established Antrim Arms Hotel boasting "Motors for Hire" and two Irish Automobile Club signs. Also incorporated in the building is a branch of the Ulster Bank. The hotel was then used as a posting depot. The other two businesses visible behind the horse and cart are McKinlay's shop and McClement's public house.

Ann Street, Ballycastle

Plate 100

An excellent view of Ann Street, one of the main business thoroughfares in Ballycastle. The Bog Oak Shop on the left belonged to John A. Macauley, who wrote "the Ould Lammas Fair". This site is now marked by a plaque. Other shops on the left include two lending libraries, one owned by Bob McCahan, who compiled a series of historic booklets on the area and the other by Coghlan's Photographic Studio. On the right is Neely's grocers; Irish Home Industries, McCaughan, grocers and a wine and spirit store. The background shows the Antrim Arms and a boot and shoe warehouse.

Bibliography

Books

Anderson R. – "The Port of Coleraine" .... *Ballycastle 1976*
Archibald W. – "The Development of Portstewart" .... *M.A. Thesis 1977*
Arnold J. – The N.C.C. Saga .... *Devon 1973*
Boyd H. A. – "Ballycastle Narrow Gauge Railway" .... *Notes*
Currie J. R. L. – "The Northern Counties Railway Vols. I and II" .... *London 1973/74*
Currie J. R. L. "The Portstewart Tramway" .... *Lingfield 1968*
Girvan W. D. – U. A. H. S. "Coleraine and Portstewart" .... *Belfast 1973*
Girvan W. D. – U. A. H. S. "North Antrim" .... *Belfast 1972*
Mullin J. E. – "The Causeway Coast" .... *Belfast 1974*
Mullin T. H. – "Coleraine in Modern Times" .... *Belfast 1979*
McCreary A. – "Spirit of the Age" .... *Belfast 1983*
McGuigan J. – "The Causeway Tram" .... *Belfast 1983*
Patterson E. M. – "The Ballycastle Railway" .... *Devon 1965*
Wilson I. – "Shipwrecks of the Ulster Coast" .... *Ballycastle 1979*

Periodicals

Coleraine Chronicle
Northern Constitution
Derry and Antrim Year Books

Others

O. S. Memoirs
Town Guides